ALCESTIS

EURIPIDES

ALCESTIS

TRANSLATED AND ADAPTED BY

TED HUGHES

FARRAR, STRAUS AND GIROUX

NEW YORK

Farrar, Straus and Giroux
19 Union Square West, New York 10003

Published in the United Kingdom in 1999
by Faber and Faber Ltd, London
First American edition, 1999

Library of Congress Cataloging-in-Publication Data
Hughes, Ted, 1930–98.
   Euripides' Alcestis / translated and adapted by Ted Hughes. — 1st
American ed.
     p. cm.
   ISBN 0-374-14920-8 (alk. paper)
   1. Alcestis (Greek mythology) Drama.   I. Euripides. Alcestis.
II. Title.
PR6058.U37A79   1999
882'.01—dc21   99-42757

DRAMATIS PERSONAE

ADMETOS, *King of Thessaly*

ALCESTIS, *Queen of Thessaly*

HERACLES, *son of Zeus by Alcmene*
and the strongest of the gods;
old friend of King Admetos

PHERES, *father of Admetos*

APOLLO, *god of music and medicine*

DEATH

PROMETHEUS, *benefactor of mankind*

IOLAUS, *attendant to Heracles*

LICHAS, *attendant to Heracles*

MAID *in the palace of Admetos*

SERVANT *in the palace of Admetos*

GOD

VULTURE

CHORUSES 1, 2 and 3, *friends of Admetos*

ALCESTIS

APOLLO

A strange thing is happening in this palace.
Incomprehensible
Only to those whose eyes
Are too narrowly trained
On the wrong causes.

A woman is dying in this house.
She is giving up her life
So that her husband can live.
And this is the day of her death.

I am partly to blame.
You may call me a god.
You may call me whatever you like.
But a god greater than I am, the greatest god,
Is guiltier than I am
Of what is happening here.

That greatest god was jealous of my son.
Think. My son was a healer.
Aesculapius. Note the name.

My son could bring the dead back to life.
He should be here today.
Aesculapius!

Perhaps you have heard this story.
The great god, the greatest of the gods,
The maker of the atom,
Is a jealous god.

A thunderbolt split heaven—and killed my son.
The dead must die forever.
That is what the thunder said. The dead
Are dead are dead are dead are dead
Forever.
They return to the pool of atoms.

Do you know what I did? I avenged my son.
I killed the electro-technocrats, those Titans,
Who made the thunderbolt.

But none of that is important
Except as a dim, forgettable cause
Of what is happening now to the dying Queen—
Alcestis.
In everything I say—remember her.
Remember what she is undergoing now,
This second and this, inside this house.
Let every woman who hears me
Imagine it is happening to her.

God punished me for my revenge.
He made me the slave
Of this woman's husband.
Me—a god—the common slave of a king.
King Admetos. However—

Admetos is a remarkable man.
A saviour of his people, an inspired prince.
A man for whom the whole country prays.

God made me his slave.
His dream became my work.
His people thought he must be divine.
The whole known world was astonished
By the prosperity of his kingdom.

Unluckily,
Admetos was doomed to die young.
But I knew how to free him from this debt.
Believe it or not, on occasion
Fate will accept a substitute. Yes,
Sometimes it is possible
To persuade Fate, vast and faceless Fate,
To accept a substitute.
My persuasion was successful. And now
Admetos can live
If only some other person, some kindred,
Will agree to give him their life
And take his place on the other side of the grave.

A difficulty!
Who do you suppose would die for him?
His old father and mother,
Two walking cadavers—
Both refused. Their voices rose to a screech.
They wanted only to live.
They set the example.

Admetos sat in his bedroom. You might say
With a terminal illness. I canvassed for him.
I was shameless. I asked everybody
Who boasted sharing the slightest family link
With Admetos. But of course
I was asking for more than a kindness.
I was asking for their heart—so to speak—
To be cut out of their chest, and stitched into his.
Only one person I did not ask:
Alcestis. His wife.

But now you know her story. Of her own accord,
She has volunteered—to give him her life.
And Death has accepted. Hers for his.

All that matters now
Is how Alcestis makes the gift of her life
And dies for her husband,
And how he accepts her gift.
This incredible gift of life.

Today, the King's new life begins.
And I stand here, at the door of his home,
To welcome it. And here it comes.
A figure of dazzling hope, a figure of power,
Bursting from the doors of death
Crammed with all the possibilities.
The new life of Admetos—welcome.

[*Enter Death.*]

DEATH

Stand aside. I have come for Alcestis.

APOLLO

Where is the new life of Admetos?

DEATH

That's none of my business.
Don't you recognise me? I am Death.
I am the one you cheated.
I wanted Admetos, her husband.
That would have been a prize worth taking.
This whole country depends on Admetos.
It seems everybody's future
Hangs on the life of Admetos—
His energy, his inspiration.
Ten thousand costly necessary projects
Wait on his word. The tricky alliances
With belligerent kings, neighbours and rivals,
Depend on his touch.
His death would have been a national catastrophe.
A nuclear bomb spewing a long cloud
Of consequences. But for me—a harvest.
You cheated me.
That's all right. I'm a good loser.
I mean, I don't mind
Postponing my winnings.
Meanwhile—Alcestis is welcome.
Now move aside.
This one's mine—and better now
While she's still so young.

Still juicy, still a beauty.
Ha ha ha! It's a long way
To the underworld
And I have my perks.

APOLLO
Let Alcestis live.
You have been slaughtering millions
For countless generations.
What are a few more years, in her case?

DEATH
You negotiated this deal.
Don't blame me.

APOLLO
I negotiated
How Admetos might prolong his life.
Why should Alcestis die to pay for it?
You are a god.
The decision is in your power.

DEATH [*Roars—a shattering roar.*]
You simpleton from the sky.
You ethereal idiot. You call me a god?

APOLLO
What god is greater?

DEATH
Don't you know how paltry and precarious
Life is? I am not a god.

I am the magnet of the cosmos.
What you call death
Is simply my natural power,
The pull of my gravity. And life
Is a brief weightlessness—an aberration
From the status quo—which is me.
I am the very body of Admetos.
Yes, horrible as I seem,
I am the admired body of Alcestis.
Their lives are the briefest concession,
My concession, a nod of permission.
As if I dozed off and dreamed a little.
I take a dream—and Admetos calls it his life.
When I awake in the body of Admetos,
He dies.
When I awake in the body of Alcestis,
She dies.
With all the power of their bodies—
They die.
And now I am awake, look at me, awake
In the body of Alcestis.

APOLLO
Yes, you could frighten a god.

[*Death roars.*]

The power of the body! Horrible!

DEATH
Yes, yes, yes, yes, yes.
The power of the body.

[*Death roars.*]

APOLLO

There are other powers. Don't forget them.

DEATH

I know.
I know what I'm up against.
You and your bright ideas, for one.
You fill the minds of human beings
With lunatic illusions,
A general anaesthesia,
A fuzzy euphoria,
A universal addiction
To the drug of their games,
Chasing a ball or power or money,
Or torturing each other,
Or cheating each other—
All that drama!
You know it.
But I cannot understand why you do it.
As far as I'm concerned, their birth-cry
Is the first cry of the fatally injured.
The rest is you—and your morphine.
That is why they call you the god of healing.
Life is your hospital and you call it a funfair.
Your silly sickroom screen of giggling faces,
Your quiverful of hypodermic syringes
That you call arrows of inspiration.
Man is deluded and his ludicrous gods
Are his delusion. Death is death is death.

APOLLO

You are not the only visitor
Arriving today at this house.
You have come for Alcestis.
Let me tell you. Another guest is due.
This other guest will take Alcestis from you.
You bluster and roar
And call yourself the gravity of creation.
Today, in this house, you will meet your master.

DEATH

Who?

APOLLO

I loathe you.
All living things loathe you.
But somebody in this universe
Can pull the darkness over your eyes too.
And today you are going to meet him.

DEATH

What are you talking about? Who is it?

[*Exit Apollo.*]

DEATH [*Roars.*]

This woman is mine.
And she is mine forever.

[*Exit Death. Enter Chorus.*]

CHORUS 1

Will Admetos want to see us, at a time like this?
I never heard this house so silent.

CHORUS 2

Is that good or bad?
Is it the careful silence of the sickroom
Where life still hangs on by a thread?
Or the silence of death? The final silence
Of the damp, cold stone?

CHORUS 3

I can't understand it.
Admetos has ransacked the earth
For specialists, witch doctors.
They have come and gone.

CHORUS 1

This is beyond medicine.
This was decided between gods.
It can be reversed
Only by a miracle. When the gods
Decide on a death
Medicine simply fails.
Then the best of doctors
Becomes a learned book or a stupid book,
That nobody can decipher.

CHORUS 3

All the hospitals on earth
Become useless monuments.
No better than pebbles on a beach.

CHORUS 2

The only real hope
Was Aesculapius, the healer,
The miracle-worker.
But God could not tolerate him.
Aesculapius died. God killed him.
God was jealous of the mighty healer.
Why?

CHORUS 3

So now there is no hope.

CHORUS 1

Everything that wealth can do
Admetos has done.

CHORUS 2

If you ask me, Admetos is a strange one
To let her die in his place.

CHORUS 3

Once she'd agreed I thought it was too late
For him to do anything about it?

CHORUS 1

Better not look at it too closely.

CHORUS 3

At some point, it seems, the heavens closed.

CHORUS 2

Even so, Admetos is a strange one.

CHORUS 1

Some things are better not talked about.

[*Enter Maid, crying.*]

CHORUS 1

What's the news?
Is she still alive?

MAID

Whatever they do, nothing helps her.

CHORUS 1

We have come to show Admetos
That his friends are standing by him
At this dreadful time. Tell him we are here.
Where is he?

MAID

He hardly knows himself.
He sits in the room, staring at her.
She is alive. And she is dead.

CHORUS 1

Have they given up all hope?

MAID

Fate is fate. This is the day she must die.

CHORUS 2

I am afraid
Admetos does not know

What his loss will mean.
He has not identified it.
He does not know what loss is.
Nothing has ever hurt him.
But when she has gone he will know it.
When everything is too late
Then he will know it.
When he has to live in what has happened.

MAID
Her women are already busy
Preparing the funeral.

CHORUS 3
Her burial will be worthy of her, resplendent.
Admetos will make sure of that.

CHORUS 2
Alcestis was unique among wives.

CHORUS 1
Alcestis was unique among women.

CHORUS 3
What other woman, anywhere on earth,
Would do what she has done?

CHORUS 1
No woman ever loved a man
As she has loved Admetos.
You hear men and women swear
They love somebody more than themselves.

They are easy words.
The act is hard. Proof of the oath is hard.

MAID

This morning, the morning of her death,
She bathed
In the fresh depth of the river.
She dipped her white, flawless body
Into the bright current.
Then out of her chest of sandalwood
She lifted her richest garment,
Her costliest jewels.
She added these beauties to her beauty.
Everybody who saw it
Choked and struggled
Between amazement and grief.
Then she kneeled—at the hearth of the house,
Before the deity of the house. And she prayed.
'Goddess:
You who have blessed my house,
Today I am going into the earth.
By this evening
I shall be nothing in the dark nothing of death.
This is the last time I shall kneel here
To ask you anything.
Goddess,
Protect my children, be their mother,
And guide them
Into strong marriages.
And let them live their lives to the utmost day,
Do not let them be plucked, like me,
Before they are ripe for falling.'

Then she went from altar to altar
Praying at each one,
And wreathing each one with fresh-cut flowers.
She prayed in silence.
Not a sob or a gasp escaped her.
That sweet, perfect face of hers—so calm.
As if evil could never come near her.

But then in her room she broke down.
She fell on the bed.
Her scream was gagged with sobs.
'It was here,' she cried, 'on this bed,
I laid myself down as a girl
And became a woman, for Admetos.
I gave him my body,
And now I give him my life.
This dear bed
Has carried the love of our lives,
The beauty of our lives.
Now I must leave you
For the first time unfaithful to you
And to Admetos.
Some other woman, some woman
Not so wound into his heart,
Not so woven into his days and years,
Will sprawl here with him
And be happy.
Happy, yes, happy, chattering about a future.
She will not even know what I looked like.'
Alcestis wept
As if her whole unlived life
Had turned into weeping.

She kneeled beside the bed and buried her face in it.
It was shocking to watch her.
To see her there, clawing at the coverlet, kissing it.
Then she got up and ran blindly away from it,
And scrambled along the wall, groping for the door.
Then flung herself back on the bed.
She was like a fly
Caught in a spider's single strand.

There her children found her.
They clung to her crying, begging her not to leave them.
And she clung to them, crying.
Then the servants burst in.
They did not know whether they should or not,
They simply did.

She thanked them all.
They could hardly see her for their tears
As she thanked each one,
And said goodbye to each one.

CHORUS 2
At least tell Admetos we are here.

[*Exit Maid.*]

And this is the woman this wealthy powerful house
Has now lost.
And what has Admetos gained—
In her place?
Life, a few years of life.
What life?

His own life. Life for himself.
If he had died he would have lost Alcestis.
Now he has lost her anyway.
From now on
As long as he lives, his life will weigh, to the grain,
Just what he paid for it.

[*Enter Maid.*]

MAID
Alcestis is trying to get up.
Admetos is supporting her,
Holding her and begging her not to die,
Not to leave him.
She is already a dead weight.
Her eyes are sunk in dark pits.
Her blood hardly moving.
Her skin cold.
She gasps for air.
And cries for light—more light.
As her light fades. 'The sunlight!'
She cries—'The sun's light! The sun's heat!
Carry me into the sun.'
This is a ghastly moment.
But Admetos wants you to share his mourning.
He wants his friends to share it.
Come in.

CHORUS 1
As usual, God is silent.
And lets it all happen.

Must it happen?
God, can't you inspire one of us
With some spark of your power—
To divert this fate from Alcestis?

CHORUS 2

Even if God answered our prayer
How would we hear it?
How would we recognise his word?

CHORUS 3

We must pray.
God only seems to be silent
Because we are so deafened by our own babble.
The powers of the creation are the powers
Of every atom in it, and all these atoms
Are slaves to laws of which we are ignorant.
Anything can happen.
We must pray.

CHORUS 1

We must pray for the spark.

CHORUS 2

And we must pray
That we shall recognise that spark
When it blazes up.

CHORUS 3

We must pray and stare into the darkness
For that spark.

CHORUS 1
Without hope.

CHORUS 2
Without expectation.

CHORUS 3
Only confident
That anything can happen.

CHORUS 1
Apollo!
Isn't Apollo the god we should pray to?
The god of healing.

CHORUS 2
The father of Aesculapius
Who could raise the dead.

CHORUS 3
Whom God killed.

CHORUS 2
How hideous
That we should be given the understanding
To know
Just how hideous it is.
Wouldn't it be better
To knot a rope round your neck
And hang yourself in the empty face of heaven?

CHORUS 3

Is it love
That has brought Alcestis to do this?
Is it love
Or something more?

CHORUS 1

Something more than love?

CHORUS 2

Never say marriage
Brings more happiness to those who marry
Than it brings pain.
Think of all the marriages you have known.
And now—look at this one.

CHORUS 3

The noblest woman
Dying in such a horrible fashion
She tortures others almost as much
As she suffers herself.
How could Admetos be made to suffer
More than he will now suffer?

[*Enter Alcestis and Admetos.*]

ALCESTIS

The sun!
The great good warmth of heaven!
Clouds
That made all our happy days

Such a bountiful procession
Of hour after hour,
When life seemed unending.

ADMETOS
The god of light up there has hard eyes.
He is watching us.
He sees only two figures,
Two clay shapes in a crypt.
Like two jars full of wine
Whose taste is their own secret.

ALCESTIS
The hills, the houses,
My place, Iolkos,
I see it all
As if I had already left it.
Here before me, and here after me.
As if I had never lived.

ADMETOS
You will live, Alcestis.
You cannot leave me. Pray.
Pray, Alcestis.

ALCESTIS
What is that black river?
Do you see the river, the glitter
Brimming among the houses?
Somebody—who is it, Admetos?
Somebody out on the river shouting for me.

DEATH'S VOICE

Alcestis!

ALCESTIS

Shouting my name.
I hear the splash of an oar.

DEATH'S VOICE

Alcestis!

ADMETOS

Ignore him, Alcestis. Pray.
Pray with me. Pray with me.

ALCESTIS

A huge cold
Coming down over me.
Huge weight,
A huge hand of ice pressing me down,
O Admetos.

ADMETOS

Fight against it, Alcestis.
Fight for your children, for me—
You are taking us all with you.
Fight. Pray.

ALCESTIS

Let me lie down.
So heavy. The strength I had
Has all gone into weight.
Goodbye, my darlings.

Remember, I loved you.
Don't waste the sun. Be happy.

ADMETOS

Goodbye! don't use that word,
Only live, live, live, live.
And stay with us.

ALCESTIS

Admetos,
You are making words meaningless.
Accept what is happening.

ADMETOS

Why? Maybe it need not happen.
You can live, Alcestis.

ALCESTIS

Admetos,
Don't be petulant with death and the gods.
These are my last words.
Don't tell me they are inappropriate
Unnecessary words.
I have given my life to let you live.

ADMETOS

No!

ALCESTIS

Be patient.
I chose this! I did not have to choose it.

ADMETOS

No!

ALCESTIS

After your death
Any man in Thessaly would have leapt
To marry me. I could have lived here,
In this house, with him.
But without you I could not live.
I am still young.
I gave you my first, best years,
And now I give you the rest. It is simple.
My life was yours when I lived.
And now, as I die, it is yours.
When I am dead, it will be all yours.
It is all of a piece, and all yours.

Who else had such good reason
To prefer your life to their own?
Your father and mother gave you your life.
And now they are old,
Now they have used their lives up,
They cannot see that they owe you anything?
Either of them could die any moment,
But the scrap of time left to them
Is more precious to them than you are.

But we are not dealing with people.
We are dealing with a god.
Admetos,
Promise me one thing.

Only a small thing.
Nothing to equal what I have given you.

I think you love our children as I do.
Admetos, let them be masters
In their own house. Do you understand me?
Do not take another wife
To be jealous of them, to persecute them,
To make their lives a curse. Do not, Admetos.
The boy might survive it.
The boy has you. But what of the girl—
A stepmother will tear her to pieces
One way or another. And the boy—
Where will he turn to for the love
Cut off in me? From her he will drink poison,
Subtle and sugared maybe, but poison.
You cannot watch over them.
These two will be in her power
And she will secretly destroy them
In the shadow of her own children.
If any can come back from the dead
Those two will bring me back
To protect them.
Promise me, Admetos.

CHORUS
He is too moved to speak.
Let me speak for him. He will keep that promise.

ALCESTIS
Admetos, promise.

ADMETOS

You have my word. I promise. I promise.

CHORUS

He is a noble man. His promise
Is made in heaven, and cannot be broken.

ADMETOS

O Alcestis,
I love you. As I have loved you alive
I will love you dead. Only you.
No other bride shall ever be mine.
There is no other woman
So beautiful, so loftily born—
Why should I need more children?
If only the gods will protect them.
They are all I have of you.
I shall mourn you, Alcestis,
Not for a year, but for my entire life.
And for my entire life
I shall detest my mother and father
Who would not throw off their carcases
To save you.
Alcestis, only you,
In the whole world, only you loved me
In word and in deed.
But weeping and groaning
Cannot fill up this chasm,
This total emptiness.
No mourning can ever be enough.
From today

This house is closed to banquets.
No more house parties. Henceforth
Laughter is forbidden beneath this roof.
For the last time I have heard merriment
Beneath this roof.
I swear this before the gods.
Alcestis, everything has gone with you.
What shall I do,
Have some sculptor make a model of you?
Stretch out with it, on our bed,
Call it Alcestis, whisper to it?
Tell it all I would have told you?
Embrace it—horrible!—stroke it!
Knowing it can never be you.
Horrible! To dream you have come back
Alive, happy, full of love as ever—
Then to wake up!

I find myself
Thinking about Orpheus—in the thick of all this.
Thinking of the impossible.
How he went down there,
Into the underworld, the dead land,
With his guitar and his voice—
He rode the dark road
On the thumping of a guitar,
A horse of music.
He wrapped himself in his voice,
Death-proof, a voice of asbestos,
He went
Down and down and down.

You remember—
He went for his dead wife
And he nearly got her.
Death let her go—on one condition.
Orpheus almost saved her. But—
He loved her too much, too helplessly.
He made a little mistake.
He made it out of love.
A tiny error—unthinking—
A glance. Think of it. Only a backward glance.
And he had done what he should never have done.
At the crucial moment.
He lost her.
Horrible!

Wait for me, Alcestis. When I die
We shall lie together forever
And ever and ever and ever.
We shall not be separated then
Till the whole universe crumbles.

CHORUS 1
We all mourn her, Admetos.
You are not alone in your grief.
Your love has a privilege, but we loved her.
And you say rightly, no mourning can ever be enough.

ALCESTIS
Children, you heard your father.
He has promised
No other woman shall ever call herself
Your mother.

No other woman shall ever rule this house
As his wife.

ADMETOS
I have promised.

ALCESTIS
Here, I hand our two children
Into your sole care. Love them
As their mother loved them.

ADMETOS
I have promised.

ALCESTIS
As she would have loved them if she had lived.

ADMETOS
If I can live without you, I shall protect them.

ALCESTIS
Time covers the grave and the grief.

ADMETOS
Only let me lie covered beside you.

ALCESTIS
Death wants only one of us. He has me.

ADMETOS
Alcestis, look at your children. Don't leave us.
How can you leave your children?

ALCESTIS

A god is deciding this, not me.

ADMETOS

Alcestis. Alcestis. O Alcestis.

CHORUS 1

She is dead.

CHORUS 2

Alcestis is dead. Your wife is dead.

CHORUS 3

Admetos,
In every marriage
One must mourn the other.
If they cannot die together
One has to live with the loss.
As for the dead one—Alcestis welcomed her death
When first she welcomed her life.
She has merely unwrapped
The gift of death her mother gave her.

ADMETOS

Words!
Don't you see what has happened?
She dreamed of the great black bird
With no eyes in its sockets
That flew at her, and pecked her—
Now I have to act like a man in control
And manage the funeral.

Friends, I am thankful you are here.
You know what we must do now.
We must sing
In defiance of this loathsome god
Who collects our bodies
With anger at our reluctance,
Like a debt collector.
But first let the year of mourning begin.
Let the people be with me in my sorrow.
Let every head be shaved.
Let every garment be black.
Let the cavalry
Crop the manes and tails of the horses.
Throughout the city
Let every stringed instrument be unstrung.
Let every flute lie breathless.

Never in my life
Shall I bury anyone
I loved so much, or who loved me more.
She died for me. Let her be honoured
As she deserves.

[*Exit Admetos, carrying Alcestis.*]

CHORUS 1
Farewell, Alcestis.

CHORUS 2
A dead woman, a falling star
With a long train

Of burning and burned-out love.
Falling into non-life.
Into endless time, endlessly falling.

CHORUS 3
No turning round. No looking back.
No changing your mind.
It has happened.
Your eyes closed, your face fixed on the direction.
You have gone through a hole in the air,
A hole in the earth, endlessly falling.

CHORUS 1
But you lived.
Your life was envied.
And when you died
Your death astonished the living.
Your death humbled all of us.
Your death
Was your greatest opportunity
And magnificently you took it.

CHORUS 2
Your love for Admetos
Converted death to nothing.
Your love
Was like a great fortress
That death could not enter—
A great fortress
For the living.
Admetos is surviving in your love.
Death cannot reach Admetos.

CHORUS 3

If we could bring you back
If there were some way
If there were means anywhere on this earth—

CHORUS 1

If there were a method in heaven
To bring you back.

CHORUS 2

If anything in life had the power
To raise you from death.

CHORUS 3

If there were as much hope
As water clings to the point of a needle.

CHORUS 1

If there were as much hope
As a single spark whirling upwards into the night
From a pyre—

CHORUS 2

If there were hope.

CHORUS 3

Alcestis, if Admetos
Should ever love any other woman
His children will hate him. And I too will hate him.

CHORUS 2

Admetos' father is contemptible—
Clinging to his bones

As if they were sacred relics.
The next lungful of air
A million times more precious than his own son.

CHORUS 3
His mother is no better.
Her gums gaping
For one more mouthful of gruel
That she cannot taste.
She has forgotten her son.
She has forgotten his name.
She cannot recognise him.

CHORUS 1
Like the beating hearts
Torn out of living crocodiles
These two refused to stop.
Bodiless, feeling nothing,
With the dust on their tongues,
They go on gulping for life.

CHORUS 3
They let Alcestis die.

CHORUS 2
Only Alcestis
Young and in her full beauty
Answered the demand.

CHORUS 3
Selfless love.
If Alcestis had not proved

That it exists—
Who would believe it could exist?

CHORUS 1

But it no longer exists.
Alcestis is dead forever.
How can we say we live in her selfless love?
How can it help anybody now?
We stand in the icy breath of her death.

[*Enter Heracles.*]

HERACLES

Greetings. Is King Admetos at home?

CHORUS 2

Heracles!
What brings you here? And today of all days.

HERACLES

Duties.
Eurystheus my master has allotted me
Yet another labour.

CHORUS 2

And where is it?
What is the task this time?

HERACLES

Distant Thrace. And the job—
Stealing horses.
The man-eating horses of Diomed.

CHORUS 1

Have you any idea what that means?

HERACLES

None at all. Thrace is new country for me.

CHORUS 1

Those horses can't be won without an army.

HERACLES

I am an army, in my small way.
Anyway, it's my job. I'm commissioned.

CHORUS 3

Diomed is the king of homicide
Who will kill you if you don't kill him.

HERACLES

So far death has never troubled me much.

CHORUS 2

But if you kill him—then what?

HERACLES

I get the horses.
Or rather Eurystheus, my greedy boss,
Gets the horses.

CHORUS 1

No easy matter, putting a bridle
Onto those heads, or a bit between those teeth.

HERACLES
So long as they're not blasting out fire
Like dragons, I don't see much of a problem.

CHORUS 5
They are man-eaters, Heracles.
And they have jaws to match.

HERACLES
Worse than lions? That's hard to believe.

CHORUS 3
Their stable walls are draped with sheets
Of coagulated blood
That they've kicked out of men. The floors
Are deep manure of mashed bones and the blood
Of trampled men. They have eaten the flesh.
Diomed feeds men to them to keep them keen.

HERACLES
He's bred them, has he? I wonder who bred him?

CHORUS 1
His father was the God of War, Ares.
He's king over that pitiless Thracian army.
Every cruelty that can be imagined—
Those heroes of his perform it.

HERACLES
The God of War's own son. You see my luck!
Either I'm pitted against monsters—

The sort that put a curfew on whole kingdoms—
Or I'm up against one son or other
Of the God of War. First—Lykaon:
They said he was more savage than his father.
Then Kyknos—who had to be tranquillised
To keep him near normal for a tyrant.
And now this terrifying fellow—another,
With horses ten times more terrifying
Than he is. Well, I take these things as they come.
That's my way, and so far it's worked.
I've never refused a fight. To tell you the truth—
I have to admit it—I like fighting.
It seems to keep me healthy.

CHORUS 2
Here comes Admetos.

[*Enter Admetos, attended by servants.*]

ADMETOS
Heracles—my old friend!
Son of Zeus himself! Welcome, welcome!
Welcome to my house.

HERACLES
Blessings on this house, Admetos.
Blessings on you and yours.

ADMETOS
Yes, yes, yes, yes. Heracles,
You are inexhaustible in your goodness.
You overflow with it.

HERACLES
Are you mourning somebody? You are shaven.

ADMETOS
We have had a death in the house.
The funeral is today.

HERACLES
Your children are safe?

ADMETOS
Thanks be to God, the children are safe.

HERACLES
And your father, and your mother?
I know they were old—
Full of a long rewarding life together.

ADMETOS
Both are still alive.
Healthier than might be expected.

HERACLES
Alcestis?

ADMETOS
Yes, Alcestis. No. Yes and no.

HERACLES
What do you mean? Yes. No. Yes and no.
Is she alive or dead?

ADMETOS
Both. Both, O Heracles!

HERACLES
A riddle! Tell me straight, Admetos.
Alive or dead—she must be one or the other.
She cannot be both.

ADMETOS
You know what happened.

HERACLES
I heard. You were doomed to die early.
She offered to take your place.
The whole world knows the story.

ADMETOS
In that case, Heracles, don't you see—
If she is doomed to die
How can I think of her as alive?

HERACLES
But any one of us can be killed tomorrow.
We don't ruin today with worrying about it.
Death can come in a twinkling, any second.
Up to that second, every second is precious,
Precious, precious life.
Death has to be ignored.
Then when it comes—mourn. Acknowledge it.
But not before it comes.

ADMETOS

Easy to say. Yes, we mourn only the dead.
But when death approaches the woman you love
More than your own life, it can't be ignored.
She becomes her living death.

HERACLES

But you are in mourning. Somebody has died.
Somebody is dead. Who?

ADMETOS

A woman of the house.

HERACLES

A foreigner? Or your kindred?

ADMETOS

She was born far off, but we loved her.

HERACLES

What was she doing here?

ADMETOS

She was an orphan.
She lived with us, after her father's death.

HERACLES

It seems like I've chosen a bad moment.

ADMETOS

Heracles, where are you going?

HERACLES

I have other friends in the region. I'll stay somewhere.

ADMETOS

Heracles, you stay here.

HERACLES

Guests are out of place in a house of mourning.

ADMETOS

Nothing can be done about the dead.
You must let me honour my guest.

HERACLES

You cannot at one and the same time mourn
And entertain me.

ADMETOS

The guest wing is apart. That's where you'll be.

HERACLES

Admetos, allow me to leave. I would be grateful.

ADMETOS

Do not humiliate me, Heracles.
Stay with me.

Show our guest
Where his rooms are. They are always ready.
Then serve him food and wine.
A hungry man, with a hero's appetite—

He's come a long way. Also make sure
The business of the funeral
Comes nowhere near him. See to it
That he forgets what's happening.
He is my dearest friend.

[*Exeunt servants with Heracles.*]

CHORUS 1
Admetos, this is not right or good.
You cannot entertain a guest with one hand
While you bury your wife with the other.
She is barely cold. You cannot do this.

ADMETOS
This living man means more to me
Than any other. How could I turn him away?
No, his arrival
Is a test of sorts. I must rise to it.
It would be too easy to throw up my hands
And tell him the funeral customs
Can't be bothered with him, today.
But I don't feel that way. I want to accept him—
Welcome him. My heart has room
To bury and mourn my wife without rejecting
My dearest friend in his need. This
Has happened strangely. What does it mean?
Anyway, I want to accommodate it
Whatever it means.
Would you prefer me to insist
That though it has happened it should not have happened?

And refuse to let it happen?
Turn my friend away, to find a bed elsewhere?
What would you think of me if I did that?
What would the world think of me?
I would despise myself.

CHORUS 2

But why, if he was so important to you,
Why didn't you tell him?
Why have you concealed your wife's death from him?
What's the point of that?

ADMETOS

If I had told him that, he would have felt boorish
Bursting in on our grief.
He would have gone away. And who could have stopped
    him?
And I would have been shamed.
As if he had shunned my home
Like a place diseased.

Simply because disaster from heaven
Has shattered my family—
That's no reason to abandon my duties
To such a friend as Heracles.

    [*Exit Admetos.*]

CHORUS 3

Hospitality
Is one of the sacred mysteries.

Accept what gift God gives—
Even the gift with an ugly wrapping.
Accept whatever befalls—
Even when it falls at a bad moment,
Inopportune,
Accept it. Every accident
Is a gift, a test. Each misfortune
Bears an opportunity,
Cradles a benefit,
If it can be accepted, and favoured,
Generously, as a guest,
As a welcome, noble guest.

CHORUS 2
There is a mystery in it.
Something is always being delivered
Out of the unknown. Often
Out of the impossible—
The hour's every moment, like a spring source,
Divulges something new.
A thought out of the heart.
A strange hand knocking at the door.

CHORUS 1
Admetos welcomed Apollo—
Any mortal might think twice
Before opening his house to a god.
Yet what came with Apollo?
Unimaginable good fortune.
Admetos is the most popular king
Ever to have reigned in Thessaly.

His reign is the luckiest—
Legendary harvests,
Flocks of incredible abundance,
A prosperous happy people.

CHORUS 3
Apollo made Admetos
The lucky charm, the living talisman
Of Thessaly. Good fortune
Blazed from his presence, as from the sun
The nurturing warmth and light.
This is why Admetos has to live.
This is why the people dread his death.
This is why he was so unwilling to die—
Unwilling to remove his blessing
From his land and people.
And yet he had it all from Apollo—
His guest.

CHORUS 2
And now you see Admetos—
Though blasted by grief
As a tree by lightning—
Admetos welcomes a new guest.

His wife, within the hour, torn from him
As one of the lungs torn from beneath his ribs,
His face harrowed with pain,
He opens his arms to Heracles.
This is high courage.
This is superhuman grace.
Greatness of spirit.

What do we mean by greatness of spirit?
We know it when we see it.
Mankind cannot attain anything
That we admire more.
Such greatness of spirit bodes well

Such greatness of spirit
Turns everything to account.

CHORUS 3
But how can this greatness of spirit
That you talk about, how can it
Turn to account the death of Alcestis?

[*Enter Admetos.*]

ADMETOS
My friends,
Thank you for sharing this with me.
My men are bringing her body.
Before we put her in the tomb
Lament her with the customary farewells.
Let the solemnities
Be formal and complete.
Let us skimp nothing.

CHORUS 3
Admetos, here comes your father,
And servants with him
Bringing funeral offerings
To go into the grave with her body.

[Enter Pheres. Enter, at the same time, bearers with Alcestis' coffin.]

PHERES

My son,
This is a dreadful day.
I have come to help you bear it.
A better wife never existed.
These gifts are for her.
I do not know why we want to bury precious
Treasures with our dead, but we do.
She gave her life for yours.
She saved you. And she saved me—
She saved me from living my last days
In mourning for my only son.
Her bravery has redeemed all women.
Alcestis,
Go to your grave blest.
Your courage saved my son.
Your generosity
Restored my house even as it collapsed
In ruins.
Be happy among the dead.
Here on earth your name is glorious.

Marriage is rarely a fortunate voyage.
The small mismatch becomes a giant rock
That shatters the vessel.
Wife and husband end up clinging to the rock
Or washed apart in the ocean.
But your wife gave you life, Admetos.

As if she existed only to give you your life.
So I bring her these gifts.

ADMETOS
You? Get away with your trash
What are you doing here?
No gift can be better than the giver
And you are worthless.
Your rubbish pollutes her death.
And your grief is meaningless.
When I was condemned to die
You snarled in my face.
You showed no more grief than a hyena.
'Die,' you said, 'hurry up and die.'
To me you said that—to your only son.
'If you have to die—die and stop whining.'
That was your grief for me.
And my mother—
If she ever was my mother—
She could only scream:
'What do you expect us to do about it?
If you have to die
Why come running to us
Asking us to die for you?
You're a man now, Admetos,
Responsible for your own debts.'
You began to shake, both of you,
At the very idea of dying—
Clinging to ivy, half of you cold in the earth,
Your feet numb in the grave,
And still you screamed for life.

'Admetos,' you wailed, 'save us.
Don't let us die. Don't kill us.
Don't ask us to die for you, Admetos.
If Alcestis wants to—that's her business.
But don't come begging to us.
We've given you enough.'

And now, look at you, death-head—
You come here, swaggering your great sorrow
For the woman you killed.
When Death made a grab at you
This is the woman you shoved into his fist.
This was your sacrificial victim—
This is your interim payment.
Rotten-gutted coward.
You think I care for my ageing parents?
This butchery of yours, here,
You see her, this dead body,
That's where all my love is, forever,
All that grateful love you might have had
Is being buried here.
Listen to me now, old man,
I detest you and your stinking mouth.
Go and cough on your wife,
Tell her what I have said.
Life spoiled you, it pampered you.
When your mother gave you life
A kingdom was added to it.
You had me, to succeed you,
Where you might have had a revolution,
The crown hacked from your body at the neck.

I made it easy for you. Easy to retire.
I let you slide back into your wealth
Like a crocodile into its lagoon.
Since that time I have honoured you both, like gods,
The gods of my house.
And how did you thank me?
'Die,' you screeched, 'clear off and die.'
Two puppets, possessed by goblins—
That's what you are.
Go and toss your sticks in a blanket
With that heartless hag of yours—
Get a new son if you can,
You will need somebody to bury you—
Because I shall leave you to the dogs.
I swear it, you Gods, do you hear me?
When these two die
Let their graves be the gullets of dogs,
Let their monuments on earth
Be the droppings of dogs.
I hate them.
'Why can't I die?' they mourn.
'Why is it so hard to die?' they whisper
As they crawl out of the lavatory.
But let death stick its face into theirs
And suddenly they're snarling, all fangs,
Full of horrible energy
Like cornered leopards.

CHORUS 1
You have said enough.
It is not good, Admetos,

53

To anger the spirit of your father.
Don't let your grief lash out so blindly.

PHERES

The royal power I gave you has gone to your head.
This is your problem.
You think you are irreplaceable.
You think your life is so priceless
Others must die to preserve it.
You think the entire country
Gets its oxygen only when you breathe in
And sings your praises as you breathe out.
You have flattered yourself
With a few years of good fortune,
A few years of lucky reputation.
And you think if you die
The whole country will die with you.
You talk to me as if I were some slave
Who works in the kitchen and sleeps with the animals.

I gave you your opportunity, your life.
Nothing obliges me to give you mine.
A man is born for himself,
Born alone, remember, to die alone.
Everything a son can expect of a father
I gave you.
When he has been given all that
Does a son knock down his father
And kneel on his chest, and jab a knife under his
        jawbone,
Yelling at him: 'Daddy,

You've kept one thing back'?
Yes, you think so. I gave you so much
I created a monster of demand.
But when I wouldn't die for you
Look what you did· you let her die instead.
You live now
Only because you let Death take her.
You killed her. Point-blank
She met the death that you dodged.
You call me a coward?
Be careful what names you use for us
Who failed to die for you, at your request.
Think of the names that will be found for you.

CHORUS 1
It's enough: abuse is the echo of abuse.
It's like the barking of dogs. Shame on you both.
It's like the screaming of apes.

ADMETOS
Let him blow himself empty.
Then I'll give him a few words.
He's beside himself.
He knows how the world will tell his story—
A tottery geriatric, horn-rimmed eyes,
Surviving on bile
And the toxins of his diseases,
Like something in a cesspit.
Who refused to die
For his son in his prime.
Let the noblest woman on this earth

Die because he dare not.
He knows he made a mistake.

PHERES

The only mistake would have been
Dying for you. The mistake
Made by that poor fool there, Alcestis.

ADMETOS

She had all her life ripe, inside her,
Unused. You are empty.

PHERES

My life might not be much in your eyes.
For me it is all I have.

ADMETOS

Cling on to it. You might outlive God,
You and that other half-corpse you keep warm.

PHERES

Why do you hate us so much?

ADMETOS

You are too greedy for life. So greedy
You sucked the life out of Alcestis—look.

PHERES

You are the cannibal. Only you
Thrive on that feast. Nobody else.
Think of it.

Every day you live she nourishes you
With her dead body.

ADMETOS
Your cowardice killed her.

PHERES
You killed her. You. You. You.

ADMETOS
Let me see the day, you Gods,
When this creature comes crawling to me
With the spittle on his chin,
Croaking for help.

PHERES
You came crawling to us
As you'll go crawling to some woman—

ADMETOS
The thought of death choked you.
You couldn't say yes or no to me.
You could only screech, like a rat pinned with a stick.

PHERES
A rat's life is all a rat has.

ADMETOS
But you can't live up to it.
You don't deserve the life of a rat.

PHERES

At least this isn't my corpse—
That you're going to bury, like a torch
To light up your own fortunate face.

ADMETOS

If ever you die, the world will despise you
For what you failed to do.

PHERES

When I'm dead the world's dead and the cat too.

ADMETOS

What loathsome sacks of refuse old men are!

PHERES

She wasn't loathsome, was she? Merely stupid.

ADMETOS

Get away.

PHERES

I am leaving the killer to hide his victim.

[*Exit Pheres.*]

ADMETOS

I curse them both.
I'll have it proclaimed throughout Thessaly.
I disown my mother and my father.
I ban them from my house.

I erase their names
From every monument and document.
They have ceased to exist.

Let us carry Alcestis to her grave

[*Exit Admetos with Alcestis, etc.*]

CHORUS 1
Who is this
Who curses his mother and his father?
Can this be Admetos? Is he mad?
Grief has made him mad.
He doesn't know what he's saying.

CHORUS 2
The Admetos that brought Alcestis to the grave
Is like the body of a rat
Trapped with bones and sinews in the trap.
He is trying to chew it off—the whole body.
Admetos is trying to gnaw himself
Free from Admetos. Admetos
Is spitting out the torn flesh and the blood
Of Admetos.

CHORUS 3
What will that leave him with?

VOICE [*Off-stage, loud*]
Let the underworld be prepared
For the bravest

That ever entered that kingdom.
Let all the shadows of the underworld
Give place
To the shadow
Of the bravest woman who ever lived.

[*Uproar of Heracles. Enter servant.*]

SERVANT
Of all the guests we've ever had here
This one is the weirdest. And the worst.
They've come from every corner of the globe
With their funny ways, lots of them difficult.
But we treat them all the same—
Banquet and bed, and they stay as long as they like.
But this fellow, and his two servants—
Who is he? He's terrible. Couldn't he
See the house is in mourning?
Couldn't he show respect?
He just crashes in
Deaf with his own din,
Like a bawling babe. Or a monster.
Any human being would have noticed
The King's distress,
And shown some consideration for us—
Accepted what we could give him
In the circumstances,
Gratefully, quietly. Not him!
'Wine!' he roars—halfway in through the door.
'Wine!'
And he lifts a whole flagon and drains it.

Six litres, without resting his glottal!
'Kill the spider down there!' he bellows
And burps into the neck of the next flagon.
Before we'd got the meat onto the table
He'd begun to dance, and sing—listen!
Strangling the song in his own drunken throat
And shouting for the actors. He wants to be entertained.
Crazy drunk in five minutes flat!
I never saw anything like it.
The maids crying and cowering.
Heracles bawling for more beef.
The house mourning Alcestis.
The hullabaloo!—
And nobody able to tell him
We are all in mourning for Alcestis—
Because the King has forbidden us
To breathe a word of it—to this drunkard.

So while they bury Alcestis
We have to humour this—whatever he is!
A wild man of the woods,
A mountain man, brought up by the bears—
This guzzler and devourer.
We wanted to go to the funeral.
Alcestis cared for us all,
She mothered us all.
The King has his weakness.
He can't quite believe
He deserves his good fortune.
His temper is not so reliable.
He's a bit of a touchy bull.

Alcestis kept him calm.
She protected us from him.
But what will happen now she's gone?
I think this new guest is a sign
Of what it's going to be like.
If this dangerous buffoon
Is the kind he likes about him—
The signs are very bad.

[*Shriek of maidservants; one runs in.*]

MAID
Heracles is killing the lion.

[*Heracles, his men Iolaus and Lichas, and all servants, maids, etc., burst in. Heracles is drunk, and draped with flower garlands.*]

HERACLES
Iolaus, you are the lion.
No weapon can kill you.
Roar, as my arrows bounce off you.
Roar. Louder. The Nemean lion was mean.
Louder. No. Listen. I am the lion.

[*Heracles roars and leaps.*]

You be Heracles. Hit me with your club.

[*Heracles roars, chases Iolaus. Maids scream as he chases everybody.*]

No, Iolaus—you're the lion and I am me.
And this is how I killed you.

> [*He strangles Iolaus, seems to tear lion skin off him,*
> *tosses body to servants, who catch it.*]

That was my first labour. My second—
The hydra—was tougher. I'll show you.
All of you—you be the heads of the hydra.

LICHAS
The monster of the bog!
Writhe and hiss. Writhe! And hiss!

> [*Lichas and Iolaus organise all the servants into a*
> *many-headed monster. Heracles grapples with it. It*
> *swarms all over him.*]

IOLAUS
Heracles grapples with the hydra
That rises from the mud of the magma
Out of which the round earth bubbled.
Seven heads belch poison gas.
Seven throats jet venom.
And every head he crushes with his club
Doubles into two new heads.
Where there were seven there are eight.
And where there were eight there are nine.

And here comes the crab, hydra's little brother,
To help the hydra.

But now I have set the forest on fire.
I have jammed a blazing branch through the crust of the
    crab
And cooked its filling. Heracles—
Break a burning branch and sear the neck-stumps.

HERACLES
Scream, hydra, scream, as your neck-stumps shrivel.
Louder, louder.

SERVANT
I must tell him. I shall have to tell him.

HERACLES
This reptile is a factory of venom.
I dip my arrows in the gall.
And the deadliest hero on earth
Becomes twice as deadly.
Now a simple scratch of my arrow
Will incinerate a rhinoceros.
But I don't need arrows
To catch the Ceryneian hind—
That bounds out of the underworld
Antlered like a stag.
There she goes.

[*Lichas plays the hind. Heracles chases it, scattering the
servants, catches it, flings it over his shoulder.*]

IOLAUS
Act four: the next labour was tougher.

HERACLES

The Erymanthian boar—
On my way there I stopped in at a party
Of creatures half-man and half-horse—
The triply-drunken centaurs.
Homicidally mad-drunk, they attacked me.
I slew a few with my new weapons—
My hydratoxic arrows.
But by horrible mischance
Wounded my dear old teacher, Cheiron—
The wisest centaur who ever galloped
On four resounding hooves.
He was immortal—
But touched with the lethal extract of my arrow
He crawled away to a deep cave.
He muffled his voice with a mountain.
He will hide his death-agony forever
Unless— There goes the boar—

[*Lichas bounds among the servants as a wild boar.
Heracles plunges after it.*]

I hunt it through the tunnels of underbrush,
I hunt it onto the crests of the hills.
I drive it into deep snow. Here it is helpless.
I wrap it in chains. My fourth labour completed
Ends the fourth act of our mighty play.

IOLAUS

Act the fifth!

LICHAS

Stench!
The Augean stables. Dung!

HERACLES

The dung spilled like fermenting glaciers
Down the valleys.
The Augean stables
Were a quiet volcano
Of slow, steaming excrement.
A solid, static, inching eruption of ordure.
I had to clean the whole place up in a day.
A trick!
I diverted two big rivers,
Alpheus and Peneus.
The Augean stables
Became a churning pool, a tide-rip.
Before sunset, the cobbles of the yards gleamed.
A brown fan opened into the seas.
But now came the birds.

IOLAUS

Act the sixth. The shite hawks!
The Stymphalian harpies. Come on, all of you.
Flap, flap, screech, and shower your bird-shit.

[*Servants, getting into the spirit of it, pelt him with
food, screeching.*]

Their faces are lances—
Spikes to nail a man to the earth
While their scalpel talons bone him out.

HERACLES

But I have a drum

[*He produces a drum.*]

To bounce the brains out through their eye-sockets.
And I have arrows
To adorn the back of their skulls with quivering crests.
The sixth labour is easy.

SERVANT

Stop! Stop! Stop!

LICHAS

Here comes act the seventh.
I am a great bull that mounted a myth.
A bull that begot a monster.
On the Queen of Crete! What a night that was!

HERACLES

The Minotaur's very own daddy.
The bull out of the sea.
What's a bull but a bag with too many handgrips?
First, the horns are handy levers
For twisting the windpipe round the spine.
Then grab its balls and hoick it clear of the earth
To disconnect the back legs from propulsion.
Then drag it out by the tail, or a handy hind hoof.
And behold
A monument of marble muscle
Is a public fountain full of goulash.

IOLAUS

What about the eighth labour?

HERACLES

The eighth? The horses of Diomed.
The man-eating horses! I see into the future.
Their bronze man-chomping teeth!
You tame these creatures
By feeding a man to them.
So I fed them with their master, King Diomed.
Then a girl could harness them.
This eighth labour is too simple.
It will be like a rest.

IOLAUS

Not the ninth!

HERACLES

The ninth! Ha! Yes! The Queen of the Amazons.
The Queen of the Amazons!
The Queen of the Amazons!
The Queen of the Amazons!

[*He whirls a maidservant about. Sings:*]

How quiet she lay at last when I took my prize.
How gentle my hands, as I lifted away her girdle.
How peaceful her face—O how shall I ever forget her?

IOLAUS

The tenth labour. The cattle of Geryon!

HERACLES

The Queen of the Amazons!

[*Sings:*]

How peaceful her face—O how shall I ever forget her?

IOLAUS

And the eleventh labour!
The apples belonging to Atlas, who held up heaven.
The apples of the orchard of the West.
Remember!

HERACLES

I remember going down into hell.

IOLAUS

The twelfth labour! That is still to come.

[*Heracles seems to see a vision—gradually more horrified.*]

HERACLES

I hear the bleating of the dead
In the valley of death.
The dead flocking towards me.
The million, million, million ghosts
Swirling about me, with their tiny mouths.
Who am I looking for?

[*Shouts, bewildered:*]

Who am I looking for?

IOLAUS
You had a strange nightmare.
A horrifying dream. Your dream became famous.
You told it and they made a play about it.
You're getting your dream mixed up with what will
      happen.
You're thinking of that play.

HERACLES
What was the play?
The madness of Heracles. Was that the title?
What did I do in that play?

IOLAUS
You did it in a dream.

HERACLES [*Now utterly horrified.*]
I see my wife. I see my dead wife.
Who killed her?

IOLAUS
It was not like that.
You climbed the mountain. Remember?

HERACLES
I climbed the mountain.

IOLAUS
You set free the Titan Prometheus.
Do you see it? He is nailed on top of the mountain,
Where the lightning strikes.

God has nailed him there.
You free him.

HERACLES [*Now as if hypnotised by Iolaus' words.*]
I free him?

LICHAS
God has nailed him there
For stealing fire from heaven and giving it to man.

HERACLES
I know the story.

LICHAS
There was more to it. And that's where you come in.
Prometheus knew a secret—
The secret of the future of God.

HERACLES
The secret of the future of God!
Why do those words make me shiver?

LICHAS
And God wanted to know what the secret was.
Prometheus would not tell him. He defied God.
So God sent the vulture.

HERACLES
Wait a minute. Give me a drink.
Prometheus and the vulture!
Yes, the vulture! The vulture!

God sent the vulture to gorge daily
On the liver of Prometheus.
There where he hangs splayed—nailed to the crag.
Because Prometheus will not tell the secret.
That is the punishment.

LICHAS
That's it.

HERACLES
I see it! I see it.
Give me another drink. I see it.
Prometheus is there, on the crag.
Look.

[*Vision opens: Prometheus splayed on the mountain crag.*]

IOLAUS
He is arguing with God.

PROMETHEUS
I have given man freedom.
When I gave him fire I gave him freedom
To re-create mankind in his own image.

IOLAUS
Now hear God.

GOD
You think you freed him? You separated him
From the illumination of heaven,

From the wisdom and certainty of heaven.
You freed him
To grope his way into the mine shaft, into the bank
    vault
Of his own ego, his selfishness
And his pride.
To grope his way into the barrow
Of his fearful solitary confinement
With no more illumination than a match.
You freed him
To grope his way into the dark maze of the atom
With no more illumination than a hope.

PROMETHEUS
I freed him to be human.
I broke the chains
That made him the slave of your laws.

GOD
You cut the nerves
That connected him to his own soul.
Perhaps that is the secret you keep from me.
When man has learned to live without his soul
I shall be redundant. That day is coming.
Man will be deaf to my corrections.
His ears will fill up with different voices.
But my vulture will still find him.

HERACLES
Prometheus, I have come to free you.

PROMETHEUS
God will never free me.

HERACLES
He knows the consequences
Of your theft of fire, but he has forgiven you.
He accepts it. God is a realist.

PROMETHEUS
He thinks I hold the secret to his future.

HERACLES
Is that a tremendous secret?

PROMETHEUS
He thinks it is, but it isn't.

[*Enter vulture.*]

VULTURE
It is! It is! It is!
I come to find it,
I come to release it—
To tear it from your liver
Where you have hidden it.
Prometheus, take your choice.
Tell the secret in plain words—
Or have it ripped from you
In lumps that make no sense
Even to mighty God,
And that only I can digest.

HERACLES
Is that a vulture?

PROMETHEUS
God's representative,
The administrator
Of his almighty judicial error.
Yes, it is the vulture.

HERACLES
Vulture! Here's a titbit for you.
A few dried molecules of the gall
From the liver of a friend of yours.
Excuse the arrow, but I have no spoon.

[*Heracles shoots vulture with arrow. Vulture bursts into
flames, and falls out of sight.*]

VULTURE
Ah!

HERACLES
I have nailed her onto the sun with a laser
More powerful than the sun.
There she can blaze and glow and be consumed
And shrivel to harmless atoms
And vanish into the great good light. Prometheus!
Your torturer is dead.

[*Heracles wrenches out the bolts that fasten
Prometheus' chains.*]

And now you are free.
But I forgot something. God promised me
That if you would tell me the great secret
I could kill the vulture and free you.
I have killed the vulture. I have freed you.
But you have not told me the secret.
I forgot to ask you.

PROMETHEUS
The story is ludicrous. It's a fairy tale.

HERACLES
Still, now you're free you'd better tell it.

PROMETHEUS
It's a prophecy.
You know that goddess of the sea—
The virgin Thetis—you've heard of her?
God is infatuated with her.
She's on his list of fruits ready to be plucked.
My secret is—or was—
If he begets on her her first son
That boy will prove greater than his father.
And will depose him. It's a fairy tale.

HERACLES
God will be deposed by his own son?

PROMETHEUS
Just as God himself, you remember,
Deposed and did away with his own father.

HERACLES
But if God knows your secret—

PROMETHEUS
He will avoid Thetis.
And that's all there is to it.
As secrets go, I'm glad to be rid of it.
I bear God no grudges. I forgive him
As he forgives me.

HERACLES
A strange tale!
God himself deposed by his own son!

PROMETHEUS
That was God's fate hidden in my secret.
Now he can avoid it. And I am free.

[*Vulture reappears, reeking with smoke, feathers
scorched to stumps, the arrow pulsing in her chest like a
strobe light.*]

VULTURE
No, I am alive and you are not free.

HERACLES
No, you are dead and Prometheus is free.

[*He fires another arrow—vulture again explodes in
flames.*]

You are dead and Prometheus is free.

[*He fires another arrow.*]

You are dead and Prometheus is free.

[*Heracles is bellowing at the top of his voice. Vulture
disappears in screeching, conflagration. Heracles
bounds to that place and fires more arrows down.*]

That's the way.
Be your own jumping cracker,
Whirl to cinders like a Catherine wheel.
Hose yourself empty of ashes like a Roman candle.
Blaze and glare to nothing
Like a pile of gunpowder.
Nothing is left of you.
Nothing is left of you.
Nothing is left of you.
You are dead and Prometheus is free.

[*Prometheus has disappeared, the visionary peak fades.
Heracles staggers, a little drunk. Bewildered.
Maidservants, etc.—all aghast.*]

SERVANT
Now will you listen?

HERACLES
What? Listen?

SERVANT
This is a house of mourning.
You are vandalising the funeral of the Queen.

HERACLES
The funeral of the Queen? Which Queen?

SERVANT
Our Queen.

HERACLES
Alcestis.

SERVANT
She is dead. Admetos
Could not bring himself to tell you.
He could not desecrate the sanctity
Of the hospitality he owed
To his greatest friend.

HERACLES
He lied to me, instead. Alcestis!

SERVANT
Our heads are shaven.
You see we are dressed in black.

HERACLES
While I was amusing myself, with my noise,
Alcestis lay dead.

SERVANT
And all of us died with her.
Admetos died. I died.
These girls died.
This is a house of death, Heracles.

HERACLES

His face was stricken. His eyes red.
I saw it—I never interpreted.
I let his words lead me by the nose and release me
To carouse and cavort like a clown.
I thought some resident stranger had died.
He let me think that.

[*Tears off his garlands, suddenly angry and sober.*]

And you let me think that—
Where is the funeral?
Where is Admetos?
Where is the body of Alcestis?

SERVANT

Outside the palace, on the north road.
You will see the tomb of black marble.
And the mourners, you will hear them long before you get
    there.

HERACLES

There is only one thing to be done.
What good are my fancy labours—
Strangling lions, beheading dragons,
Pitching homicidal mesomorphs
Out of their strutting careers.
These are paltry work.
If Zeus was my father, what am I doing
Wasting my divine inheritance
On this rabble?

I need a challenge worthy of my father.
I need to get my double nelson
On an immortal neck.
Every labour so far has served
Only to prepare me for this.
Death has taken Alcestis.
How if I were to wrench Alcestis
Out of the grip of Death? And open her eyes
As if she had only fainted for a moment?
Blacked out—for a first glimpse
Of nothingness.
This will prove me a friend in need, to Admetos,
And to Alcestis.
This will prove to Admetos
That his respect for me was not misplaced.

I must hurry.
Death will be there already
Lapping up the blood that pours
From the sacrificed beasts.
Then while the mourners wail
And try to convert the pain of grief
Into physical wounds on their own bodies,
Death will bend over her.
He'll embrace her.
He'll plant his cold kiss on her dry lips—

Then he will feel, as he bends there,
My arms around his neck.
If I'm too late, no matter.
I shall go down through the earth—

And if I fail to overtake them
I shall penetrate
The palace of the God of Hell
And his poor unfortunate Queen, Persephone.
They will not refuse me.
I shall pluck Alcestis, like a stalk of asphodel,
From the tossing crowd of new shadows.
And I shall hand her back to Admetos,
This lord of hospitality
Who made me so welcome, even in his worst hour,
Who had to tolerate my drunken antics,
Who gave me licence to do as I pleased
Though he was dumb with grief.
Who gave me his house
When the light of it, the holy flame,
Had just flickered out.

He did all this—simply to honour me.
In all Thessaly, in all Greece
There is nobody to touch him
For loyal friendship, for kingly behaviour.
A man of this temper
Shames every other man or woman
To match him in nobility of spirit.
No one will ever say Heracles alone
Failed to respond in kind.

[*Exit Heracles. Enter Admetos.*]

ADMETOS
This house! This horrible empty box!
A huge grave.

In it, one huge wound—that took the life
And is now cold.
A numbed mouth with swollen lips
Left behind by a pain too huge to utter.
Pain—dark pain
Instead of the light—pain.
No refuge anywhere in me
From this fire, this huge dark single flame,
That caresses my whole body.
I think of cool soil,
A mask over my face,
A weight of stillness over my body,
A darkness
In which she lies next to me—her lips
Maybe only an inch from my lips.
Forever.

CHORUS 1
You should hide this grief inside your house.

ADMETOS
Alcestis!

CHORUS 2
Yes, you have suffered. And you will suffer.

ADMETOS
Alcestis! Alcestis!

CHORUS 3
This helps neither the dead nor the living.

ADMETOS

The mind tries to be its own doctor.
But every thought of her
Rips off the dressings, sets the blood flowing afresh.
We should never have married.
Men who have never married
Keep their nerves inside their own skin.
The nerves of the married man,
His very entrails, all his arteries
Are woven into the body of his wife—
And into the bodies of his children.
Let the groom beware.
Yes, and let the bride beware too.

CHORUS 1

What has happened had to happen.
Men have endured far worse, with silence.
Some have even managed a smile.
Half the world's husbands lose their wives.
Now live on—to learn what that means.

ADMETOS

Why did you restrain me
When I made the effort to die there
Beside her, and to lie
In the one tomb?
What is there about my life
That is preferable
To what she chose?
If I had chosen that—
I would have all I want.
I would have her beside me.

Look at the stones of this house.
Sitting in their place,
Just as they sat, unmoved, through her entire life.
I feel like a stranger.
As if I had never seen them before.
These same stones
Vibrated to the flute, the dances and the songs
That brought Alcestis and me from our wedding.
I remember that feast—
The speeches and the toasts and the faces
Shining with joy to have such a chance
To be so joyful.
They recited your lineage, Alcestis,
And wove it into mine,
So cleverly. With so much laughter!
So much confidence. So many blessings.
So much time!
So many decades ahead of us.

This house is nothing but a trinket
Surviving the body that warmed it.
It should be burned
So nobody else can carry it off
Into a new life.
A life ignorant of Alcestis.
Or else I should sit here, and go mad,
Like a madman in a cave,
A recluse in his cave, with his secret.

CHORUS 1
You have been too fortunate.
You have been spoiled.

Your wealth, your happiness
Have stupefied you.
Suffering, the inescapable sorrow
Of living in the same world as death,
Has come as a surprise.
As if it never came to any man before you.
As if it had chosen you unfairly.
How childish!

ADMETOS

My wife is happy.
Life is agony and she is free of it.
What greater good fortune can there be
Than to escape the worst that life can bear—
As she has escaped it.
I have to face it.
I dodged my fate. I who should be dead
Now have to face this life.
At last I understand what that means.
How can I enter my own house?
Who will greet me there?
Her empty chair. The imprint of her body
On our bed. And the children
Crying for their mother.

And where else can I go? Wherever I go
I shall see weddings,
Dancing excited women and girls—
I shall see her friends among them.
I shall feel like an animal
With a fatal wound—
Wanting only to crawl off into a hole.

And what will be said about me?
Everywhere the same:
'There he goes.
How can he shame to stay alive,
That coward
Who was so afraid of death
When his father and mother refused
To die in his place he cursed them.
When he saw death coming, like an arrow,
He dodged behind his wife.
He let her die for him, to save his life.'
Don't ask me to live!
When every man or woman who knows my story
Can deal me this wound, and will deal it.
Even if they do not say it, they will think it.
How can I live with this?

CHORUS 2
You know about Fate.
You know about what we call
Necessity.
What must be will be.
Among all the gods that we name,
Among all the powers of the earth,
Nothing is omnipotent
Except this
Simple Necessity.

CHORUS 3
Man is quite helpless against it.
Medicine preens and promises
But doctors perform
Only where Necessity lets them.

CHORUS 1

Greater than all the gods
It has no shape. Cannot even
Be represented by an image.
It has no temple, no cult.
Prayers or sacrifices cannot affect it.
Cruel, blank, pitiless,
Its movement is only
What must be will be.

CHORUS 3

What force are you, Necessity?
We have felt your might.
Spare us. You give God a bad name.
God can operate only where his will
Happens to coincide with yours.
Otherwise his plans are obliterated,
As we often see,
Like a vineyard under a flow of lava.
Necessity—
Your motion is both lightning
And too slow to detect.
Like the whole of creation
Revolving in time.

CHORUS 1

Admetos—
If this is a goddess, this Necessity,
She holds you now in her embrace.
Forget your futile pleading for Alcestis.
Stop wailing to have her brought back.

Your new wife, Necessity,
Will not permit it.
Mourn Alcestis, but like a true grave
Keep quiet about it.
Life is what we can snatch
From the smiles of Necessity.
Either die, or be happy—
At least be cheerful.

CHORUS 2

The greatest, the most gifted, all perish
Under the earth.
They have only one regret:
The days they wasted multiplying laments
Over what could not be helped.
The hours they spoiled
Puffing up their gravity
With being gloomy.
Indulging their misfortunes with long faces,
Giving their bad luck the run of their days.
Now they know they were fools.

CHORUS 3

Necessity could not frighten Alcestis.
We pray to Necessity to spare us,
But we pray to Alcestis
To give us courage to live—as if death
Were no more than the outline of life,
The outline of a shadow on a wall,
Maybe the shadow of a dancer, a reveller,
Somebody cheerful.

Pray to her, Admetos.

Let us all pray to Alcestis.

Alcestis, give us your courage

To meet Necessity with a cheerful face.

Alcestis! Alcestis!

Give us the courage to live.

[*Enter Heracles with a veiled woman.*]

HERACLES

Admetos,

A man must speak out his anger against his friends.

If he buries it under his tongue

It will poison the sources of his affection.

I thought I was your friend.

When I arrived here, I found you mourning.

But you lied to me.

You hid the truth—that Alcestis was dead.

Somehow you made me believe

You were burying some stranger.

You let me think it was nothing of importance.

You welcomed me, feasted me,

You let me pour wine down my throat to all the gods

Till the room spun—

You led me to this sacrilege, Admetos.

I desecrated the funeral of Alcestis.

You tricked me into it.

You were an accessory to my crime.

It was a crime.

But I understand.
I see your dilemma. I pity you. I know
My arrival set you a painful problem.
I might have been justified, even so,
In rushing away from this house
When I knew how I had polluted it.
I thought better of it.
I left the house—but for a different purpose.

See here.
This woman is very special.
I want you to guard her for me here
Till I come back
Leading the horses of Diomed
After I've killed their owner.
If by some decision of heaven
I fail to reappear—
The woman is yours.
Accept her as my gift.
And I tell you, Admetos,
I did not win her easily.

I happened to walk in on a contest of athletes.
The prizes were good.
Horses for the long-distance runners
And the sprinters,
But for the boxing and wrestling
Oxen, and this woman, believe it or not,
Thrown in, as a bonus
To the winner of the finals.
It all seemed too good to miss.

And, as you see, I did not miss it.
Look after her, Admetos.
I have not stolen her from some father or husband.
She's the prize of a clean, hard fight.
And you might yet live to be glad I won her.

ADMETOS
You understand, Heracles,
Why I hid my wife's death from you.
Let's say no more about it.
The fact of her death is more than enough
To make a madman
Forgive me. And forget it.
But I must ask you, Heracles,
For a little further understanding
Concerning this woman.
The very sight of her, standing there
Where Alcestis stood, is agony to me.
Heracles, let somebody else protect her.
Somebody untouched by new bereavement,
Who won't be hurled back into grief
By her mere presence.
I can't bear to look at her.
How could I keep her here,
Displacing Alcestis?
Don't ask me, Heracles.

And where could I lodge her safely?
This house is full of young men, well-fed and idle.
Look how young she is—
I could never guarantee my protection
However I might punish the guilty.

You are asking me
To do what is maybe impossible, anyway.
I could never keep her apart
In my own chambers,
Sleeping in the bed of Alcestis
Think what the mouths would make of that.
How I leapt from my wife's grave
Into the bed of a new woman—
As if I had let my wife die in my place
Only to be free to do that.
I can already hear Alcestis—
I hear her actual voice
Crying to me underground. No. No.
I cannot let Alcestis be dishonoured
Even in a lying rumour.

Whoever you are, I am sorry.
You are too like Alcestis.
I know the eyes of bereavement
Fixed in their focus on what's missing
Find it everywhere.
It's a delusion, but none the less painful.

Heracles, take her away.
I know she's not my wife, but looking at her
I see only my wife.
I had begun to get control of myself.
Take her away.

Aaah!
Now I know what my life has become.

CHORUS 1

When misfortune presses on a man
The whole earth shifts its position
To add its weight,
And lock the misfortune into place.
But this too has to be borne.

HERACLES

If I had the strength to bring your wife
Back from the dead, my friend,
Be sure I would have done it.

ADMETOS

I believe you, Heracles.
But why even think of such a thing?
It is too well known: the dead do not come back.

HERACLES

You can mourn too much—and hurt life.
Remember your duty to life. Be strong.

ADMETOS

Easy for the strongest man on earth
To tell me to be strong.

HERACLES

A whole life of mourning would avail nothing.

ADMETOS

I don't mourn for a reason, or for duty.
I mourn because everything in me mourns.
Everything in me loved her.

HERACLES

Losing the loved one is the worst grief.

ADMETOS

Losing her—I have lost everything.

HERACLES

You have lost an extraordinary woman.
No man could have loved her
As much as she was worth. Not even you.

ADMETOS

How am I going to live? I don't want to live.

HERACLES

Your grief is too raw, and grief is speaking.
Time will heal it.

ADMETOS

Time will bring death, and death will bury it.

HERACLES

Admetos—a new life, a new wife.

ADMETOS

How can you say that, in this house,
To me?

HERACLES

You cannot live out your entire life a widower.

ADMETOS

The woman meant for my bed—is not alive
Anywhere on this earth.

HERACLES

How can this help Alcestis?

ADMETOS

It helps me
To know that it is so. And will stay so.

HERACLES

A noble remark.
But many would call it folly.

ADMETOS

Though she is dead, I only hope to die
If ever I betray her.

HERACLES

This is not loyalty. This is suicide.

ADMETOS

Better I were dead than faithless to her grave.

HERACLES

In that case
This woman is safe with you. Admit her
To your chambers. There she will be safe.

ADMETOS

No, Heracles. No. No. No.
Haven't you heard one word of what I've said?

HERACLES

Admetos, this 'No' of yours
Is a serious mistake, believe me.

ADMETOS

And what about my 'Yes'?
That would kill me. Would that be an error?

HERACLES

Admetos,
Listen to me. Take her.
Do you hear what I say, Admetos?
Do you hear my meaning? Take her.
Your friend Heracles, the son of Zeus,
Is trying to tell you something. Take her.
This courtesy to her
Might outweigh all duties
In the time of your greatest need.

ADMETOS

Did you have to accept her?
Couldn't you have given her back to the judges
And kept the cattle?

HERACLES

Your friend's triumph, Admetos, is your prize.

ADMETOS

A fine phrase. Now let the woman go.

HERACLES

If she must. But first—look in her face.
Then tell me if she must.

ADMETOS

Forgive me, Heracles—I am your friend,

But I am a king, the husband of Alcestis.

This woman must go.

HERACLES

The circumstance

That gives my words this firmness

Is not so slight, Admetos.

ADMETOS

Very well.

My friend's pleasure, Heracles, is my pain.

HERACLES

Indulge me a little—this much, this one time.

ADMETOS

Heracles, to you I yield.

[*To servants:*]

Lead her to my chambers.

HERACLES

No—I'm sorry, Admetos.

Let this be my day.

I will not hand her over to slaves.

ADMETOS

Then take her in yourself.

HERACLES

She is yours, Admetos.
I will not hand her to anyone but you.

ADMETOS

Let her go in alone. I will not touch her.

HERACLES

Your right hand. This one. Lead her—

ADMETOS

This is neither the time nor the place for your strength.

HERACLES

It is for you to be strong.
My strength is the strength you are rejecting.
Welcome your guest. Close her hand in yours.
Look at her—you are not beheading a Gorgon
Who will turn you to stone.
You hold her?

ADMETOS

Yes, I hold her hand.

HERACLES

Protect her, Admetos. Cherish her.
And one day you will say
Heracles, son of Zeus, was a noble guest.
And now, Admetos, look at her. Look at her face.
Tell us if she resembles Alcestis
As you thought she did.
Forget your sorrows. Look at happiness.

[Admetos lifts the woman's veil.]

ADMETOS

You Gods in heaven!
Give me the words!
Heracles, have you hypnotised me
To see what I cannot believe?

HERACLES

No hypnosis, Admetos.
This is your wife, Alcestis.

ADMETOS

Or a ghost? Conjured up for a moment.
You can do anything, Heracles—
But don't trick me.

HERACLES

I am your friend, remember.
The son of Zeus, not a conjuror.

ADMETOS

I buried her today. Alcestis?

HERACLES

This is your true and only wife, Alcestis.

ADMETOS

Can I embrace her? Will she speak to me?

HERACLES

She is yours.
All you had thought you had lost—she is here.

ADMETOS

Alcestis!

HERACLES

May no watching god be jealous.

ADMETOS

Heracles!
Your labours, your entire glorious life
Are nothing to this.
May Zeus your father
Guard your life
As you have given me mine,
As you have restored my wife's life to her.
But how did it happen?

HERACLES

I fought with the God of Death.

ADMETOS

Was that the clean hard fight?
How did you find him? Where?

HERACLES

Beside the grave.
I surprised him, and trapped his neck in a lock.

ADMETOS

Will she speak?

HERACLES

Three days of silence.

It is a small payment.

Three suns will cleanse her.

Take her to your chambers. And in future

Honour your guests.

Goodbye, Admetos.

My master, Eurystheus, sits on his throne in Argos,

Thinking of me

And of the man-eating horses,

And of Diomedes, the War-God's child.

ADMETOS

This house is yours, Heracles. Stay with us.

HERACLES

Another time. My work has to be done.

ADMETOS

Be fortunate

In the future as in the past.

Come back to us in triumph.

Throughout my kingdom

Let all give thanks.

Let all rejoice—

Dancing, music, feasting, bonfires.

We have taken the full measure of grief
And now we have found happiness even greater.
We have found it and recognised it.

CHORUS 1

Incessantly the gods
Manipulate the fortunes of mankind—
Bringing great events
To conclusions that were unexpected.

CHORUS 2

Nothing is certain.
What had seemed inevitable
Comes to nothing.

CHORUS 3

And now
See how God has accomplished
What was beyond belief.

CHORUS 1

Let this give man hope.